FROM TEXAS TO NEW YORK

by Scarlett Jones
illustrated by Alphonse Azpiri

Harcourt

SCHOOL PUBLISHERS

Printed in China

ISBN 10: 0-15-350529-X
ISBN 13: 978-0-15-350529-4

Ordering Options
ISBN 10: 0-15-350334-3 (Grade 4 Below-Level Collection)
ISBN 13: 978-0-15-350334-4 (Grade 4 Below-Level Collection)
ISBN 10: 0-15-357521-2 (package of 5)
ISBN 13: 978-0-15-357521-1 (package of 5)

5 0 7 0 0 10   00G   1C 11 10 00

Corey Franklin gazed out the window of the plane. He watched the rolling hills and plains of Texas fade away. Next to him, his father leafed through a newspaper. His mother studied a book called *Finding Your Way Around New York City*.

"Are you excited about your new job?" Janell asked her husband.

"Excited, and a bit nervous, too," Elston replied.

Corey was not the least bit excited. In fact, he tried very hard not to burst into tears. He was not happy about leaving Texas. The thought of moving to a big city like New York was even worse.

After a long journey, the big jet finally touched down. Corey uneasily stared at the skyline of New York outside the window.

Elston Franklin's new company had sent a taxi to take the family to their new home. They would live in an apartment in Manhattan. Elston would begin his new job in one week. Corey's mom had decided to go back to school to become a nurse. It was the end of summer, so Corey and his mother both had exactly one week before school started.

Corey thought about when he had said good-bye to his best friend. When Janell saw her son's sad face, she put her arm around him and comforted him. "It will be okay," she said sympathetically. "We'll all have to get accustomed to living in a big city."

Their new apartment was up on the twentieth floor! Corey thought about his home in Texas. It had a front door and a back door that led into a backyard. Now he had to take an elevator just to get inside his house.

That night, Corey was trying to sleep. He heard loud sirens and cars endlessly honking their horns. Corey put his pillow over his head. "This is terrible!" he thought. "I'll never get any sleep." He climbed out of bed and wandered into the kitchen where he found his mother and father.

"Looks like we are not the only ones who can't sleep," chuckled Elston.

"I have a fabulous idea," said Janell, pulling out her guidebook. "Let's plan what we'll see tomorrow on our first day in New York."

Bright and early the next day, the family started out for the Empire State Building. They decided to take the subway, but they got hopelessly lost. "This subway is awfully confusing," Corey said anxiously. "Are we going to spend all day down here?"

"Don't worry, we'll figure it out soon enough," Elston replied calmly as they continued to ride the trains. "Sometimes when you get lost, you discover new places."

Soon they heard the subway conductor announce, "Next stop, 161st Street, Yankee Stadium."

"Yankee Stadium, Dad?" said Corey.

When they stepped off the subway, they recognized Yankee Stadium. It is one of the most famous ballparks in the country. "I guess there is a game today, judging by all the people here," said Janell.

"We're in luck because the Yankees are playing against our hometown team, the Rangers," Elston said.

That afternoon, they rooted for their team from Texas. They rooted for the home team, too. It turned out to be a fantastic day after all.

That night Corey sent an e-mail to his best friend.

Dear Peyton,

Today was our first day in New York. We spent most of the day lost on the subway. We ended up in a place called the Bronx. The best part was that we went to a baseball game, and we got to see the Yankees play the Rangers. It was incredibly cool. Tomorrow we're going to try to get to the Empire State Building again.

Bye for now,
Corey

The next day, the Franklins set out again for the Empire State Building. This time they ended up on the other side of town. They huddled together on the sidewalk, studying Janell's guidebook.

"It looks like we're at the Museum of Natural History," said Janell. "This sounds like a pretty cool place to see."

"Well, let's go in," Elston replied. "We can always visit the Empire State Building tomorrow."

They spent the day walking through the museum. Corey was amazed at all the fascinating things there were to see.

Later that day, Corey wrote to his friend again.

Dear Peyton,

Lost again today on the subway. This time we ended up at a really cool museum. We saw dinosaur bones and a big blue whale. The museum even had a planetarium. We watched a show about planets and stars. New York City is a pretty cool place, even if it is noisy and crowded and confusing.

Corey

That night, Corey fell asleep so quickly that he didn't even hear the car horns honking outside his window.

The next day, Elston absolutely had his heart set on going to the Empire State Building. He was going to get there by subway, too!

This time, they ended up at Central Park. Janell could hardly keep from laughing. "As long as we're here, let's see the sights!" she suggested cheerfully.

They spent the afternoon at the huge park that is right in the middle of the city. There are ponds, a zoo, horse-and-buggy rides, and a big lawn for picnics. It turned out to be a really good day.

Corey had a lot to write about that night.

Dear Peyton,

Lost again for the third day on the subway. This time we ended up at this great park. There was a fabulous zoo, but the best part was the Great Lawn. People come there to play ball and run with their dogs. We bought a picnic lunch and ate there, too. Tomorrow, Dad is going to try to get us to the Empire State Building again. Who knows where we will end up!

Bye for now,
Corey

The next day, Elston decided they would forget about the Empire State Building and go to the Statue of Liberty instead. Luckily, they got lost and ended up at the Empire State Building!

Looking out over the city from the top of the famous skyscraper, Corey said, "I think I'm actually going to like living here."

"Me, too, and I think I know how to get us home on the subway!" said Elston. Everybody burst out laughing. There were so many opportunities in New York. Corey and his family were ready to discover all of them.

Think Critically

1. How would you describe Corey?

2. How did Corey feel about moving away from Texas? How did his feelings change?

3. Where did Corey and his family end up when they took the wrong subway the first time?

4. What word on page 5 shows that Janell was trying to make Corey feel better about moving to New York?

5. Which of the sights that Corey's family saw would you most like to see yourself? Why?

 **Social Studies**

Make a Brochure Choose one of the places that Corey's family visited in New York City and find out more about it. Make a brochure that would make others want to visit the place, too.

School-Home Connection Share Corey's story with family members. Then discuss what it is like to move to a new place. Together make a list of some ways to become familiar with a new place.